I0191407

Sunlight In The Shadows

Poems from a Woman Finding Her Way

Lini Mathew

/ BookLeaf
Publishing
India | USA | UK

Made with ❤ on the BookLeaf Publishing Platform
www.bookleafpub.in
www.bookleafpub.com

Dedication

*"For my Children and for every Reader who finds a piece
of themselves within these Poems"*

Preface

There comes a time in every journey when the map fades, the compass wavers, and the road ahead blurs into the unknown. In those moments, we are left with only ourselves—our fears, our hopes, our questions—and the quiet, persistent voice that whispers, keep going. This collection of poems was born in such moments. Each piece is a fragment of that search: for meaning, for direction, for the self we sometimes lose in the noise of the world. As you read, you may find lines that echo your own thoughts, memories, and dreams. You may discover that a poem here knows you better than you know yourself. If that happens, let it linger. Let it speak. Because sometimes the way forward is not found in answers, but in recognising yourself in another's words. This book is not a guide, nor is it a destination. It is simply a companion for the road—a reminder that you are not alone in your search, and that somewhere between the first page and the last, you might just find a piece of yourself.

Acknowledgements

This book would not have been possible without the many souls who have walked beside me—some for a moment, some for a lifetime. To those who loved me, challenged me, encouraged me, or even broke me—you have each left footprints on my path, and in one way or another, these poems are yours too.

To my family and friends who believed in my words even before I did, thank you for reminding me that my voice matters. Your faith has been my anchor on days when doubt tried to pull me under.

To the quiet strangers whose kindness lit the way, and to the readers who will hold these pages in their hands—you are part of this journey now. My hope is that somewhere in these lines, you will find a reflection of your own courage, your own beauty, your own way forward.

And lastly, to life itself—for every twist, turn, detour, and blessing—thank you for teaching me that the way is not always straight, but it is always worth walking.

1. The Road I Left Behind

As I was sitting by the road, watching my life drift by,
I once had wealth, much power and the stars in the sky.
But after everything I gained, I came to realize
I'd never known love - the ultimate Prize.

So there I sat, by the roadside bare,
Leaving behind the world that didn't care.
The Day transformed to night and with it thankfully
sleep,
Silence and sorrow, is all that I reaped.

You came by, like a Calm in the Stormy Grey,
And softly, faithfully, chose to stay.
You took my hand to change my fate—
With love that came just in time, and not late.

Together we walked, no more alone,
With hearts entwined, a life our own.
And now I know, with all my soul,
I'll never again sit by that road.

2. Mysterious Prince Charming

The memory of those deep brown eyes,
Piercing the depths of my very soul,
The first time ever, so many years ago...
Walking up to me...My heart couldn't but skip a beat!
Reminisce of John Travolta in "Greased Lightnin"!!
Could he be my Prince Charming?

"Lady stay away or you gonna burn" said a well wisher,
"Coz he's already taken, more so a bit of a Heckler!"
Oh! Damn! But the memory of those deep brown eyes,
Piercing the depths of my very soul.
You got my heart skipping a beat,
How I wished he was my Prince Charming...

Years passed by in the blink of an eye,
Destiny decided where we were meant to fly.
The bumpy roads, though lonely were bravely taken,
My life at a standstill and then...

Oh! Damn! But again those deep brown eyes,
Piercing the depths of my very soul...
As he walked up to me now...older...wiser...
My heart like yesteryears not forgetting to skip a beat!
He Walked over like "Greased Lightnin"...
My Mysterious Prince Charming!!

3. Stripped Bare But Not Disgraced

As you are stripped bare of what you thought defined you,
Your lustrous hair, your beauty,
Your haute couture and your rambunctious personality.

You begin to experience God's unfathomable love and mercy,
By just being still in his comforting embrace.
You soon realize when there's nothing to hide behind,
That God made you in his likeness, pure and kind.

That your beauty within remains untouched and unfazed,
Only because of his unfailing love and Grace.

4. The Last Kiss of the Butterfly

As I was standing in the forest, silent and deep,
Where shadows gather and secrets sleep,
A golden ray broke through the night—
A butterfly danced in radiant light.

Wings of yellow, brushed with flame,
I watched it circle me, soft as a mane.
Resplendent in its perfect grace,
It kissed my soul and lit the place.

In its glow, I innocently bloomed anew,
Like a fragrant flower kissed by the morning dew.
I was wrapped in its beauty, lost in time,
Held by something almost divine.

But just as quietly as it came,
The Butterfly vanished, light without a name.
If only I had known that day,
That it would be the last time that it flew away.

I'd have held it close, a heartbeat more,
And kissed its wings as they began to soar.
For in that moment, however small,
I had the rarest gift of all.

5. The Sunrise in your eyes

I dream of waking up when the morning glows,
Beside the one my every heartbeat knows—
To feel the stillness before the light,
Wrapped in your arms from the velvety night.

As the dawn will tiptoes through the blinds,
I'll be watching lost in time,
Not at the sky in painted hues,
But in your eyes....my forever muse.

Before the world begins to stir,
Before the first soft song of the birds,
I wish to rise where warmth begins—
Not from the sun, but from your skin.

Why do I need the golden skies above,
When I can wake to your light and love—
To tangled sheets and sleepy sighs,
And that beautiful sunrise in your eyes.

— For the man who makes my morning worth waking up to.

6. Love Eternal That Cradled My Heart

In the quiet between two heartbeats, I heard your call,
One music to the ear, the other fierce enough to take a
fall —
A boy and girl, appeared on wings of grace,
I held you both the world stood still, as time slowed its
pace.

Two tiny mouths, two searching eyes,
Rooted to me with newborn cries.
Your breaths became my lullabies,
Your need, my deepest prayer.

As you drank from my life's quiet stream—
A love so vast, I couldn't dream.
It wasn't pain, it wasn't mundane,
But something so divine that I can't explain.

Your little fingers curled around my skin,
Nourishment flowing warm from deep within—

Not just food, but my soul I gave,
To fill the tiny hearts I longed to save.

One nestled near my beating chest,
The other in my arms at rest—
And I like the moon between two stars,
With love that heals a thousand scars.

I saw eternity in your eyes,
The girl with dreams, the boy who flies.
Two halves of me, so full, complete—
Two melodies in perfect beat.

The world may never understand
How full I felt with each small hand—
But in that moment, calm and blessed,
I found my Eternal Love, at my breast.

7. The Home That Sheltered Me

As I stand in the doorway,
the walls still breathing my name,
sunlight spilling across the floor
like a memory that refuses to fade.

These rooms have heard my laughter,
soaked my tears into their quiet corners,
and held me safe in storms
That I thought would never pass.

These windows knew my dreams,
watched me grow beyond their frames,
and the Walls—oh, the Walls—
still carry the scars of my many Falls.

I have to leave now,
not because I love it less,
but because its gift was always this—
to give me wings

and trust I'd use them.

Yet, as I step away,
I know I am woven into its story,
as it is woven into me,
a shelter that will forever
be my first sky.

8. Love in the Wild

I've swiped through princes, frogs, and ghosts,
chatted with "entrepreneurs" who still live with their
folks.
One man sent selfies from his gym,
another's was clearly half naked from a swim.

Memories of coffee dates where he forgot my name,
and one whose mom - a colleague — bless him, but... no,
not the same.
There was the poet who rhymed love with dove,
and the biker who said commitment just "wasn't his
glove."
Then came another who thought he was "Jack"
who promised me that I was so hot that the Titanic
wouldn't have "Sank"

Yet through every awkward laugh and mismatched plan,
I still believe in the magic of meeting "my man."
Because somewhere out there, amid this dating parade,

is someone who'll love me — and not just for the Vindaloo I made.

9. Up in Smoke (Almost)

I packed my dreams and my overstuffed suitcase,
headed for the US at a jet-set pace.
Security lines, coffee in hand,
I was ready for take-off to that promised land.

There she was — the traveller bold,
with nicotine cravings worth more than gold.
"Boarding now!" the gate agent cried,
but she puffed away, arms open wide.

The plane could leave, her seat could go,
but give up a smoke? Oh, heavens, no!
We all waited, tapping feet in despair,
while she finished her "last one" with a holiday flair.

America was calling, the runway was clear,
but her cigarette romance was holding us here.
When she finally strolled in, no shame, no regret,
I thought, that's a love story I'll never forget.

10. Punchlines & Punch-Backs of a Cancer Comedian

Cancer knocked, all serious and grim,
but I answered the door with a wink and a grin.
It brought its gloom, its heavy frown,
I brought bad jokes and wore a sparkly crown.

While it tried to scare me with doctor-speak,
I cracked puns that made the nurses shriek.
Chemo days? I called them my "spa retreat,"
complete with gossip and hospital treats.

It thought it could win with doom and dread,
but I hit back with giggles instead.
And when the scans came back all clear,
I raised my glass — "Not today, dear!"

Now I tell the tale, and folks all agree
Humour's the cure that worked for me.
Because cancer detests laughter — it can't take the heat,
and I'm living proof that a punchline can beat.

11. Her Majesty - Queen Sheba

Upon her throne which is the living room chair,
Her Majesty rules with a regal stare.
Her whiskers twitch, her tail held high,
as if the whole world should bow and comply.

She surveys her realm with amber eyes,
where humans serve and obedience lies.
The food must be fresh, the water just so,
or the royal paw will swiftly say "no."

At 3 a.m., her kingdom awakes,
as she orders a feast or demands head shakes.
Her purr is the hymn, her meow the decree,
and somehow, we all serve happily.

For though she's a queen in fur and pride,
she seldom curls on my lap, the crown set aside.
And in that moment, I gladly concede —
Sheba's not just my cat... she's my queen indeed.

12. Super Sumathi

Super Sumathi vrooms in at dawn's first light,
armed with a broom and unstoppable might.
She sweeps like a cyclone, dust dare not stay,
and rearranges things her perfect way.

She hums while she works, a mysterious tune,
sometimes morning, sometimes afternoon.
Ask her to pause? She'll shake her head —
"There's no rest till the dirt is dead!"

She knows every corner, every stubborn stain,
and somehow finds teaspoons I thought were slain.
Mixing coffee to make stronger tea
Juicing Avocado Seed and not the pulp...now that's
Comedy.

Super Sumathi, queen of my clean domain,
you fight the mess, I reap the gain.
And though I joke about her comical reign,
truth is — without her, I'd go insane.

13. Always around the Corner

Not just a cousin, but a brother in heart,
there since the beginning, right from the start.
Through laughter and trouble, through joy and tears,
you've walked by my side for all these years.

When life felt heavy, you lifted the weight,
turning my storms into something of fate.
No judgment, no questions, just steady and true,
a quiet strength I could lean on in you.

We share the same roots, the same family tree,
but it's your kindness that means the most to me.
And I know, come what may, as life twists and bends,
you'll always be more than my cousin —
you're my forever friend.

14. To My Dad in Heaven

I look for you in the morning light,
in the quiet of stars that crown the night.
Your voice still echoes, calm and near,
whispering comfort I long to hear.

Though heaven holds you far from my hand,
your love still guides me where I stand.
In quiet moments, I feel you stay,
walking beside me, lighting my way.

I'll carry your lessons, your laughter, your grace,
until we meet in that timeless place.
And Dad, if you can hear me above the skies —
I'm sending my love on the wings of my sighs.

15. The Strongest Woman I Know

When the world was still young around her,
and dreams had barely taken flight,
a shadow called cancer tried to claim her light —
but it didn't know the fire it faced that night.

She stood, not with armor or sword in hand,
but with faith, with courage, and the will to stand.
She met each day like a warrior queen,
turning pain into power, fear into serene.

Years have passed, yet her spirit remains,
unbroken by trials, untouched by chains.
She carries her scars like medals of gold,
each one a story of battles bold.

And I, her child, watch and believe,
that strength is something we choose to weave.
For she showed me that hope can grow —
in the toughest soil, in the coldest snow.

Mom, you're my lighthouse, my compass, my song,
you taught me that love makes the weak become strong.
And I live each day with the courage you gave,
because you showed me what it means to be brave.

16. The Flute Player

He stood in the hush of a silver dawn,
A shadow where the sunlight yawned,
Fingers resting on slender wood,
Breathing music only my soul understood.

Each note curled through the morning air,
Like whispered secrets tangled there,
They slipped past reason, past my guard,
And found the place I kept most barred.

His eyes did not seek mine to claim,
No grand gestures, no spoken name,
Just the flute's low cry, the lilting art,
And suddenly—he had my heart.

I followed the melody, breathless, unsure,
Each phrase a promise, tender, pure,
And in that song, I came undone—
For I loved the man... and the music he spun.

17. The Saviour's Shadow

You came to me on my darkest night,
A sudden flame, a burst of light,
You held my hand, you eased my fear,
I called you friend... I drew you near.

But hidden beneath your gentle guise,
A blade lay cold, behind your eyes,
And while I trusted, blind and true,
You struck the blow I never knew.

The wound was deep, the ache was real,
No easy time, no magic heal,
Yet in the ashes, I found my way,
To lay my anger down one day.

For chains of hate would bind me fast,
While love and grace can outlast,
So though you broke what we once had—
I forgave you... and I'm glad.

18. Tarzan... and Thank Goodness I'm Not Jane !

Back in the day, you swung from trees,
Hair all wild and all scraped knees,
You'd pound your chest, "Me Tarzan! You Jane!"
And I'd giggle like sunshine after rain.

Fast-forward years—oh, what a twist,
No jungle drums, no vine-swing bliss,
Just a man in jeans with a thinning mane,
Still kind of loud... but not the same.

We chatted polite, we laughed at the past,
I realised some crushes aren't meant to last,
For vines can break, and dreams can fade,
But oh, the fun that childhood made!

So thank you, Tarzan, for that sweet refrain—
But in this life... I'll skip the Jane.

19. Late-Bloom Sisters

We grew up side by side, yet far,
Two hearts drifting under different stars,
Childhood passed in separate streams,
Each chasing our own quiet dreams.

But time, that gentle, cunning thread,
Wove paths we never thought to tread,
And somewhere past the rush of years,
We found a bridge through laughter and tears.

Now you are not just blood, but friend,
A constant I can trust to the end,
For life may scatter, twist, and bend—
But sisters find their way again.

20. Niece by Birth, Daughter by Love

You came into my life with a smile so small,
A spark of sunshine, a laugh to enthrall,
At first, you were my cousin's child—
Sweet, curious, endlessly wild.

But love has a way of changing names,
Of blurring the lines, of shifting frames,
I held you close, I saw you grow,
Through scraped knees and dreams you'd sow.

Some bonds are written in more than blood,
They're carved in trust, in tears, in good,
And somewhere along that winding lane—
You became my child, not just in name.

So niece you were, but daughter you'll stay,
In my heart, in my life, in every way.

21. The Day My Name is Only an Echo

When my voice is gone, let them say—
She fought through night to claim her day,
She bore her scars like crowns of fire,
Her will unbent, her heart entire.

Let them speak not of an easy road,
But of the storms she shouldered and owed,
Of how she stood when the ground would shake,
And rose again each time she'd break.

May they tell my story, bold and true,
A flame that burned, a sky that grew,
A warrior's soul, unbound, unchained—
Whose courage lived where fear was slain.

And if my name fades into dust,
Let my deeds be the thing they trust,
For I leave behind, in blood and breath,
A legacy that outlives death.

In whispered winds, let echoes play,
Her laughter lingered, come what may,
With every tear that graced her face,
A testament of strength, of grace.

So carve my tale in stone and light,
Remember her drive, her endless fight,
For in the shadows where whispers blend,
Her spirit soars, it will not end.

www.ingramcontent.com/pod-product-compliance
Lightning Source LLC
Chambersburg PA
CBHW050959030426
42339CB00007B/407